The pond is Frog's home.
He hops in the pond.
Frog swims this way and that.
Frog likes to eat bugs.

2

The trees are Moth's home.
Moth likes to brag a lot.
She thinks she is the best.

One time Moth went to see Frog.
"Do you know the old oak tree?" said Moth.
"Yes, I know that tree," said Frog.
"There is a web in that tree," said Moth.
"The web has a big bug in it!"

3

"I will race you for it," said Moth.
"I can go fast and I will win."
"You are not as fast as you think," said Frog.
"We will see," said Moth.

4

Frog hops from pad to pad to get there.
Moth stops to take a bath.

5

6

Frog jumps from log to log.
Moth stops on a log by the path to rest.
Frog keeps on and will not stop.

At last, Frog gets to the tree.
He jumps up and gets the bug.
Then Moth gets there.
Moth sees that the bug is not there.

7

8

"Thank you for the bug," said Frog.
"Next time you will not brag.
To win the race you must keep the pace!"